EXPLORING WORLD CULTURES

Afghanistan

Joanne Mattern

Cavendish Square
New York

Published in 2017 by Cavendish Square Publishing, LLC
243 5th Avenue, Suite 136, New York, NY 10016

Copyright © 2017 by Cavendish Square Publishing, LLC

First Edition

Website: cavendishsq.com

This publication represents the opinions and views of the author based on his or her personal experience, knowledge, and research. The information in this book serves as a general guide only. The author and publisher have used their best efforts in preparing this book and disclaim liability rising directly or indirectly from the use and application of this book.

CPSIA Compliance Information: Batch #CW17CSQ

All websites were available and accurate when this book was sent to press.

Cataloging-in-Publication Data

Names: Mattern, Joanne.
Title: Afghanistan / Joanne Mattern.
Description: New York : Cavendish Square Publishing, 2017. | Series: Exploring world cultures | Includes index.
Identifiers: ISBN 9781502621504 (pbk.) | ISBN 9781502621528 (library bound) | ISBN 9781502621511 (6 pack) | ISBN 9781502621535 (ebook)
Subjects: LCSH: Afghanistan--Juvenile literature.
Classification: LCC DS351.5 M37 2017 | DDC 958.1--dc23

Editorial Director: David McNamara
Editor: Kristen Susienka
Copy Editor: Rebecca Rohan
Associate Art Director: Amy Greenan
Designer: Joseph Macri
Production Coordinator: Karol Szymczuk
Photo Research: J8 Media

Printed in the United States of America

Contents

Afghanistan is a country in southern Asia. It is surrounded by land on all sides. The capital of Afghanistan is Kabul. Afghanistan is the twelfth-largest country in Asia.

Mountains cover most of Afghanistan. The country also has **plains** and rocky deserts. Rivers flow from the mountains into the northern plains. The weather in much of Afghanistan is very hot and dry.

About thirty million people live in Afghanistan. The country's population includes several different **ethnic** groups. Afghans speak many different languages. Most people in Afghanistan live in the country, but there are also several large cities.

People in Afghanistan like to spend time with their family and friends. They celebrate festivals and holidays. Afghans also love sports and games. This nation has seen some difficult times and terrible wars, but its people do their best to live normal lives.

An Afghan vendor sells sweets and pickles in a busy marketplace in Kabul.

Afghanistan covers 251,827 square miles (652,230 square kilometers). It is completely surrounded by the countries of Iran, Turkmenistan, Uzbekistan, Tajikistan, Pakistan, and China.

This map shows the important cities in Afghanistan, as well as the countries around it.

The Hindu Kush mountain range lies in the northeast and central parts of the country. Some of these mountains are very high. The Baba Mountains are also located in the central part of Afghanistan. The Paropamisus Mountains lie in the west.

A Pass Through the Mountains

The Hindu Kush is very hard to cross because the mountains are so high. An opening called the Khyber Pass lets people travel through the mountains.

Trucks travel on the Khyber Pass.

Crops grow on Afghanistan's northern plains. These plains are watered by rivers that flow down from the mountains. The nation's most important rivers are the Helmand, Kabul, and Hari. Much of the southern part of the country is covered by rocky deserts, including the Margow and Rigestan.

FACT!

The temperature can reach over 100 degrees Fahrenheit (38 degrees Celsius) in Afghanistan's deserts.

7

People first lived and farmed in Afghanistan about 100,000 years ago. In 1219 CE, Genghis Khan invaded the country. After his death, Afghanistan broke into smaller states. Each state was ruled by a chief.

Giant statues of Buddha had stood in Afghanistan's Bamiyan Valley since the sixth century, but they were destroyed by the Taliban in 2001.

Over the next few centuries, several different groups ruled Afghanistan. A group called the Pashtuns took control in 1747. During the nineteenth century, Great Britain and Russia fought over Afghanistan. The country finally became

Genghis Khan

Genghis Khan was one of the most powerful conquerors in history. At one time, his empire stretched from China to eastern Europe.

A portrait of Genghis Khan

independent in 1919. It was a monarchy for many years. In 1973, Afghanistan became a **republic**.

In the late 1990s, a group called the Taliban took over Afghanistan. The Taliban had many strict rules. In 2001, the United States and Great Britain went to war with the Taliban.

FACT!

Afghanistan's government has changed more than forty times in its history.

9

Afghanistan's official name is the Islamic Republic of Afghanistan. Its government is made up of three parts. The executive branch includes an elected president and two vice presidents. The

President Hamid Karzai opens Afghanistan's Parliament in 2011.

president appoints men and women to a **cabinet**.

The legislative branch is called the National Assembly. It is made up of the House of Elders and the House of the People. The president appoints the members of the House of Elders.

The Afghan citizens elect members of the House of the People. The National Assembly makes laws and approves **treaties**.

In 2004, Hamid Karzai became the first elected president of the nation.

Afghanistan follows sharia, or Islamic, law. The judicial branch makes sure laws are fair. Afghanistan's Supreme Court has nine judges.

Capital City

Kabul is the capital of Afghanistan. It is the largest city in the nation. More than three million people live there.

Kabul's grand Presidential Palace

Most Afghans are farmers. They grow apples, apricots, melons, grapes, and raisins. Afghanistan also produces wheat and rice.

Farmers in northern Afghanistan check their beehives.

The most important flower in Afghanistan is the poppy. This flower is used to make illegal drugs such as opium and heroin. The government is trying to cut down on opium production, but growing it allows Afghans to make a lot of money.

Lapis lazuli is a beautiful blue gem. The finest lapis lazuli in the world is found in Afghanistan.

Afghans also mine natural gas, salt, and a mineral called chromite. Many Afghans work in the service industry. About 40 percent of Afghans sell goods, drive buses and taxis, or work in restaurants, banks, offices, and hospitals.

Money

Afghanistan's money is the afghani. One afghani can be divided into smaller units called puls. Afghani paper money is very colorful and shows important Afghan sites.

Afghanistan's colorful paper money shows important buildings and places.

13

Many animals and plants live in Afghanistan. Wild sheep and goats live in the high mountains. Snow leopards, brown bears, and wolves live in the thick forests. Herds of gazelle and oryx live on the plains.

Although much of Afghanistan is dry, some wetlands provide homes for many different animals.

A small rodent called the jerboa survives in the desert by getting most of its water from the food it eats. Snakes, lizards, and scorpions also live in the desert. Geese and cranes live in Afghanistan's wet **marshland**. Brown trout and other fish swim in the country's rivers.

More than 450 types of birds live in Afghanistan.

Pine, cedar, oak, and maple trees grow in Afghanistan's mountains. Apple, almond, and pear trees grow along the rivers. There are also many different flowers in this country, including poppies, tulips, irises, and lilies.

Save the Snow Leopard!

The snow leopard is one of the rarest mammals in the world. Only about 150 of these big cats are left in Afghanistan.

The beautiful snow leopard

About twenty-nine million people live in Afghanistan. The largest group is the Pashtuns. They make up almost 40 percent of the country's population.

A Pashtun nomad herds a flock of sheep.

Tajiks are the second-largest group. They originally came from Iran. Most Tajiks live in the eastern mountains and are shepherds and farmers. The third-largest ethnic group is the Hazaras. They live mostly in central Afghanistan. Uzbeks live in the north. Other ethnic groups include Aimaks, Balochs, and Turkmen.

Pashtunwali

The Pashtuns share a code of rules called Pashtunwali. The code explains how people should act. Pashtunwali encourages sharing, courage, respecting others, and protecting a family's honor.

Afghanistan's many different ethnic groups mean that the country has a lot of different cultures and traditions. However, these different groups also fight over their differences.

FACT!

About twenty different ethnic groups live in Afghanistan. Each group is divided into tribes, clans, and families.

Lifestyle

Family life is the center of society. Many generations live together in one house. The oldest male in each household is the head of the family. Men are in charge of business and make most of the rules. Women are

This Afghan father and son wear a mix of traditional and modern clothing.

in charge of the household and raising children. Children are taught to respect their elders and put their family first.

FACT!

Only about 25 percent of Afghan women and 55 percent of men can read and write.

For years, because of war, many children did not attend school in Afghanistan. Girls could not attend school when the Taliban ruled the country. This began to change in 2002. Today, people are building new schools and making sure everyone can get an education.

Afghan Weddings

Most marriages are arranged between families. When an Afghan girl gets married, she becomes part of her husband's family. The families celebrate with parties, good food, and music.

A happy bride and groom travel to their wedding, along with their families.

Religion

Afghanistan's official religion is Islam. Followers of Islam are called Muslims. Muslims follow the teachings of the Prophet Muhammad. These are written in a holy book called the Quran.

The Blue Mosque was built in Mazar-i-Sharif in the fifteenth century.

There are two groups, or **sects**, of Islam. About 80 percent of Afghans are Sunni Muslims. About 19 percent are Shia Muslims. Both Sunnis and Shias pray in **mosques**. Muslims pray by kneeling on prayer rugs and bowing their heads to the floor.

The Five Pillars of Islam

All Muslims are expected to follow the Five Pillars of Islam: saying, "There is no God but Allah, and Muhammad is His messenger," praying five times a day, donating to the poor, fasting each day during the holy month of Ramadan, and making at least one journey to the holy city of Mecca.

Thousands of men gather for the noon prayer in Kabul's central mosque.

Only 1 percent of Afghanistan's people do not follow Islam. These people include Jews, Sikhs, Hindus, and Christians.

FACT!

The leader of a mosque is called an imam.

Afghanistan has two official languages. These languages are Pashto and Dari. Pashto is spoken by the Pashtuns. Dari is spoken by other ethnic

This sign includes both English and Pashto writing.

groups, including the Tajiks and Hazaras. In 1936, the government declared that Pashto was the official language of the country. However, so many people spoke Dari that it remained important. In 1964, Dari was also named an official language of Afghanistan.

22

Children learn both Pashto and Dari in school. Dari is also used in business. Many Afghans speak two or more languages. In addition to Pashto and Dari, they might speak Uzbek, Turkoman, Baluchi, or another language. Some people also learned to speak English, French, Russian, or other languages if they went to school before the Taliban came to power.

Write It Down

Both Dari and Pashto are written in Arabic script. The words read from right to left on the page.

Afghans have created many beautiful pieces of art. The country is known for its colorful wool carpets. These carpets are made by hand and include many different colors and patterns. Each ethnic group or region has its own traditional patterns.

A group of men dance a lively *attan* at a public gathering.

The *rubab* is Afghanistan's national instrument. The rubab looks like a banjo. Lutes and drums are also popular.

Music and dance are very important. The *attan* is the national dance of Afghanistan. Men stand in a circle and move their feet very quickly as they clap their hands. The attan is often performed at religious festivals and weddings. Afghan women also perform dances that tell stories about their lives.

Happy New Year!

Nauroz is the most important festival in Afghanistan. It is celebrated on March 21. That date is the first day of spring. It is also the first day of the new year in the Persian calendar.

Fun and Play

Afghans have to work hard. Many of them have difficult lives. However, they still enjoy a chance to have fun. Dancing and playing music are popular ways to spend time. Afghan

Boys enjoy a game of soccer in a field outside of Kabul.

men also get together at teahouses. They drink tea and share news with one another.

Soccer is a popular game. Children play soccer in the streets or in stadiums in cities like Kabul. Other popular sports include wrestling, and a type of stickball called *topay-danda*.

FACT!

Chess is a popular game in Afghanistan.
A chess game can last all day!

Buzkashi is the national sport of Afghanistan.
Teams of men play on horseback. Buzkashi has
been played for about eight hundred years.

No Sports Allowed?

Sports were not allowed in Afghanistan when the Taliban ruled the country. It was even against the law to watch a game! Now Afghans are rebuilding their sports teams.

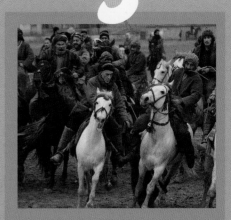

A team of men charges forward on their horses in a game of *buzkashi*.

Food

Food is an important part of everyday life in Afghanistan. The most popular food in Afghanistan is rice. Afghans prepare rice in many ways. They serve it plain or with meat. They also season it

Oshi afghani is a tasty dish made of chicken, chickpeas, and carrots served over rice.

with different spices. Pilau is a popular mix of rice, meat, vegetables, and spices.

Many fruits and nuts grow in Afghanistan. These foods are a big part of the diet. Afghans eat cheese, eggs, chicken, and lamb.

Sit Down and Eat

Afghans don't usually sit at a table to eat. Instead, they sit around a large cloth or carpet on the floor to enjoy their meal.

An Afghan family enjoys a traditional dinner in their home.

Naan is a popular flatbread. It can be eaten with yogurt or other foods. Afghans use naan to scoop up their food.

The most popular drink in Afghanistan is tea. Green tea is popular in the north. Black tea is popular in the south.

Glossary

cabinet   A group of advisors to the leader of
                  a country.

ethnic   Related to people who have a
                  common national or cultural tradition.

marshland   Land that is wet all of the time, such
                  as swamps or bogs.

mosques   Muslim places of worship.

plains   Large areas of flat land with few trees.

republic   A state where power is held
                  by the people and their
                  elected representatives.

sects   Groups of people with different
                  religious beliefs than the larger group.

treaties   Agreements between countries.

Find Out More

Books

Whitehead, Kim. *Afghanistan*. Philadelphia, PA:

Mason Crest, 2016.

Wittekind, Erika. *Afghanistan*. Minneapolis, MN:

ABDO Publishing Company, 2013.

Website

National Geographic Kids: Afghanistan

http://kids.nationalgeographic.com/explore/

countries/afghanistan/#afghanistan-blue-mosque.jpg

Time for Kids: Afghanistan

http://www.timeforkids.com/destination/afghanistan

Video

Afghanistan's Children: Small Voices, Big Dreams

https://youtu.be/if252_bBix4

This video interviews Afghan children about the

difficulties of life during war and their dreams.

Index

About the Author

Joanne Mattern is the author of more than 250 books for children. She specializes in writing nonfiction and has explored many different places in her writing. Her favorite topics include history, travel, sports, biography, and animals. Mattern lives in New York State with her husband, four children, and several pets.